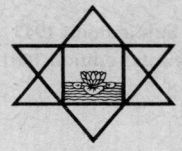

SRI AUROBINDO

The Four Aids

SRI AUROBINDO ASHRAM
PONDICHERRY

First edition 1945
Second edition 1991

ISBN 81-7058-267-9

© Sri Aurobindo Ashram Trust 1991
Published by Sri Aurobindo Ashram Publication Department
Printed at Sri Aurobindo Ashram Press, Pondicherry
PRINTED IN INDIA

CONTENTS

3
The Four Aids

27
A Letter to a Disciple

32
Extracts from Letters

Publisher's Note

"The Four Aids" is the first chapter of Part One of *The Synthesis of Yoga*. On 24 November 1945 it was published along with several letters as a pamphlet. The text was preceded by this "Prefatory Note":

This highly valued chapter of 'The Synthesis of Yoga' is offered to the seekers and those interested in spiritual life on the occasion of the November Darshan of Sri Aurobindo and The Mother as a first fruit of the newly started press of the Ashram. The composition was largely done by the young Sadhakas and Sadhikas of the Ashram though in the later stages of the work they were naturally assisted by others.

The 'Synthesis' is widely demanded by seekers of Yoga and our gratitude is always deep to anyone who is able to lend his "Arya" file or the typed copy of the work. It will yet take a long time before the whole 'Synthesis', which may be bigger than The Life Divine, is printed in book form. But until then it will certainly be a great satisfaction to possess the first chapter of the Yoga of Works, the chapter entitled The Four Aids, which lays down the basic framework, the four essential conditions, of spiritual life.

At the end we have given a few pages from Sri Aurobindo's letters, a literature yet largely unpublished and much sought after. 'A Letter to a Disciple' and 'Extracts from Letters' given here appeared recently in 'The Advent'. But, published along with The Four Aids, they may make a valuable supplementary reading.

The Synthesis of Yoga has since been issued in its entirety. But "The Four Aids" and the letters with which it was published in 1945 remain excellent introductions to Sri Aurobindo's Yoga. It gives us great pleasure to reissue this text for the use of "seekers and those interested in spiritual life".

THE FOUR AIDS

The Four Aids

Yoga-siddhi, the perfection that comes from the practice of Yoga, can be best attained by the combined working of four great instruments. There is, first, the knowledge of the truths, principles, powers and processes that govern the realisation – *śāstra*. Next comes a patient and persistent action on the lines laid down by this knowledge, the force of our personal effort – *utsāha*. There intervenes, third, uplifting our knowledge and effort into the domain of spiritual experience, the direct suggestion, example and influence of the Teacher – *guru*. Last comes the instrumentality of Time – *kāla*; for in all things there is a cycle of their action and a period of the divine movement.

*   *   *

The supreme Shastra of the integral Yoga is the eternal Veda secret in the heart of every thinking and living being. The lotus of the eternal knowledge and the eternal perfection is a bud closed and folded up within us. It opens swiftly or gradually, petal by petal, through successive realisations, once the mind of man begins to turn towards the Eternal, once his heart, no longer compressed and confined by attachment to finite appearances, becomes enamoured, in whatever degree, of the Infinite. All life, all thought, all energising of the faculties, all experiences passive or active, become thenceforward so many shocks which disintegrate the teguments of the soul and remove the obstacles to the inevitable efflorescence. He who chooses the Infinite has been chosen by the Infinite. He has received the divine touch without which there is no awakening, no opening of the spirit; but once it is received, attainment is sure, whether conquered swiftly in the course of one human life or pursued patiently through many stadia of the cycle of existence in the manifested universe.

Nothing can be taught to the mind which is not already concealed as potential knowledge in the unfolding soul of the creature. So also all perfection of which the outer man is capable, is only a realising of the eternal perfection of the Spirit within him. We know the Divine and become the Divine, because we are That already in our secret nature. All teaching is a revealing, all becoming is an unfolding. Self-attainment is the secret; self-knowledge and an increasing consciousness are the means and the process.

The usual agency of this revealing is the Word, the thing heard (*śruta*). The Word may come to us from within; it may come to us from without. But in either case, it is only an agency for setting the hidden knowledge to work. The word within may be the utterance of the inmost soul in us which is always open to the Divine. Or it may be the word of the secret and universal Teacher who is seated in the hearts of all. There are rare cases in which none other is needed, for all the rest of the Yoga is an unfolding under that constant touch and guidance; the lotus of the knowledge discloses itself from within by the power of irradiating effulgence which proceeds from the Dweller in the lotus of the heart. Great indeed, but few are those to whom self-knowledge from within is thus sufficient and who do not need to pass under the dominant influence of a written book or a living teacher.

Ordinarily, the Word from without, representative of the Divine, is needed as an aid in the work of self-unfolding; and it may be either a word from the past or the more powerful word of the living Guru. In some cases this representative word is only taken as a sort of excuse for the inner power to awaken and manifest; it is, as it were, a concession of the omnipotent and omniscient Divine to the generality of a law that governs Nature. Thus it is said in the Upanishads of Krishna, son of Devaki, that he received a word of the Rishi Ghora and had the knowledge. So Ramakrishna, having attained by his own internal effort the central illumination, accepted several teachers in the different paths of Yoga, but always showed in the manner and swiftness of his realisation that this acceptance was a concession to the general rule by which effective knowledge must be received as by a disciple from a Guru.

But usually the representative influence occupies a much larger place in the life of the sadhaka. If the Yoga is guided by a received or written Shastra, – some Word from the past which embodies the experience of former Yogins, – it may be practised either by personal effort alone or with the aid of a Guru. The spiritual knowledge is then gained through meditation on the truths that are taught and it is made living and conscious by their realisation in the personal experience; the Yoga proceeds by the results of prescribed methods taught in a

Scripture or a tradition and reinforced and illumined by the instructions of the Master. This is a narrower practice, but safe and effective within its limits, because it follows a well-beaten track to a long familiar goal.

For the sadhaka of the integral Yoga it is necessary to remember that no written Shastra, however great its authority or however large its spirit, can be more than a partial expression of the eternal Knowledge. He will use, but never bind himself even by the greatest Scripture. Where the Scripture is profound, wide, catholic, it may exercise upon him an influence for the highest good and of incalculable importance. It may be associated in his experience with his awakening to crowning verities and his realisation of the highest experiences. His Yoga may be governed for a long time by one Scripture or by several successively, – if it is in the line of the great Hindu tradition, by the Gita, for example, the Upanishads, the Veda. Or it may be a good part of his development to include in its material a richly varied experience of the truths of many Scriptures and make the future opulent with all that is best in the past. But in the end he must take his station, or better still, if he can, always and from the beginning he must live in his own soul beyond the limitations of the word that he uses. The Gita itself thus declares that the Yogin in his progress must pass beyond the written Truth, – *śabda-brahmātivartate* – beyond all that he has heard and all that he has yet to hear, – *śrotavyasya śrutasya ca*. For he is not the sadhaka of a book or of many books; he is a sadhaka of the Infinite.

Another kind of Shastra is not Scripture, but a statement of the science and methods, the effective principles and way of working of the path of Yoga which the sadhaka elects to follow. Each path has its Shastra, either written or traditional, passing from mouth to mouth through a long line of Teachers. In India a great authority, a high reverence even is ordinarily attached to the written or traditional teaching. All the lines of the Yoga are supposed to be fixed and the Teacher who has received the Shastra by tradition and realised it in practice guides the disciple along the immemorial tracks. One often even hears the objection urged against a new practice, a new Yogic teaching, the adoption of a new formula, "It is not according to the Shastra." But neither in fact nor in the actual practice of the Yogins is there really any such entire rigidity of an iron door shut against new truth, fresh revelation, widened experience. The written or traditional teaching expresses the knowledge and experiences of many centuries systematised, organised, made attainable to the beginner. Its importance and utility are therefore immense. But a great freedom of variation and development is always practicable. Even so highly scientific a system as Rajayoga can be practised on other lines than the organised method of Patanjali. Each of the three paths of the *trimārga*,[1] breaks into many bypaths which meet again at the goal. The general knowledge on which the Yoga depends is fixed, but the order, the succession, the devices, the forms must be allowed to vary; for the needs and particular impulsions of the individual nature

---

[1] The triple path of Knowledge, Devotion and Works.

have to be satisfied even while the general truths remain firm and constant.

An integral and synthetic Yoga needs especially not to be bound by any written or traditional Shastra; for while it embraces the knowledge received from the past, it seeks to organise it anew for the present and the future. An absolute liberty of experience and of the restatement of knowledge in new terms and new combinations is the condition of its self-formation. Seeking to embrace all life in itself, it is in the position not of a pilgrim following the highroad to his destination, but, to that extent at least of a path-finder hewing his way through a virgin forest For Yoga has long diverged from life and the ancient systems which sought to embrace it, such as those of our Vedic forefathers, are far away from us, expressed in terms which are no longer accessible, thrown into forms which are no longer applicable. Since then mankind has moved forward on the current of eternal Time and the same problem has to be approached from a new starting-point.

By this Yoga we not only seek the Infinite, but we call upon the Infinite to unfold himself in human life. Therefore the Shastra of our Yoga must provide for an infinite liberty in the receptive human soul. A free adaptability in the manner and the type of the individual's acceptance of the Universal and Transcendent into himself is the right condition for the full spiritual life in man. Vivekananda, pointing out that the unity of all religions must necessarily express itself by an increasing richness of variety in its forms, said once that the perfect state of that essential unity would come when each man had his own religion, when not bound by sect or traditional form he followed the free self-adaptation of his nature in its relations with the Supreme. So also one may say that the perfection of the integral Yoga will come when each man is able to follow his own path of Yoga, pursuing the development of his own nature in its upsurging towards that which transcends the nature. For freedom is the final law and the last consummation.

Meanwhile certain general lines have to be formed which may help to guide the thought and practice of the Sadhaka. But these must take as much as possible the form of general truths, general statements of principle, the most powerful broad directions of effort and development rather than a fixed system which has to be followed as a routine. All Shastra is the outcome of past experience and a help to future experience. It is an aid and a partial guide. It puts up signposts, gives the names of the main roads and the already explored directions, so that the traveller may know whither and by what paths he is proceeding.

The rest depends on personal effort and experience and upon the power of the Guide.

* * *

The development of the experience in its rapidity, its amplitude, the intensity and power of its results, depends primarily, in the beginning of the path and long after, on the aspiration and personal effort of the sadhaka. The process of Yoga is a turning of the human soul from the egoistic state of consciousness absorbed in the outward appearances and attractions of things to a higher state in which the Transcendent and Universal can pour itself into the individual mould and transform it. The first determining element of the siddhi is, therefore, the intensity of the turning, the force which directs the soul inward. The power of aspiration of the heart, the force of the will, the concentration of the mind, the perseverance and determination of the applied energy are the measure of that intensity. The ideal sadhaka should be able to say in the Biblical phrase, "My zeal for the Lord has eaten me up." It is this zeal for the Lord, – *utsāha*, the zeal of the whole nature for its divine results, *vyākulatā*, the heart's eagerness for the attainment of the Divine, – that devours the ego and breaks up the limitations of its petty and narrow mould for the full and wide reception of that which it seeks, that which, being universal, exceeds and, being transcendent, surpasses even the largest and highest individual self and nature.

But this is only one side of the force that works for perfection. The process of the integral Yoga has three stages, not indeed sharply distinguished or separate, but in a certain measure successive. There must be, first, the effort towards at least an initial and enabling self-transcendence and contact with the Divine; next, the reception of that which transcends, that with which we have gained communion, into ourselves for the transformation of our whole conscious being; last, the utilisation of our transformed humanity as a divine centre in the world. So long as the contact with the Divine is not in some considerable degree established, so long as there is not some measure of sustained identity, *sāyujya*, the element of personal effort must normally predominate. But in proportion as this contact establishes itself, the Sadhaka must become conscious that a force other than his own, a force transcending his egoistic endeavour and capacity, is at work in him and to this Power he learns progressively to submit himself and delivers up to it the charge of his Yoga. In the end his own will and force become one with the higher Power; he merges them in the divine Will and its transcendent and universal Force. He finds it thenceforward presiding over the necessary transformation of his mental, vital and physical being with an impartial wisdom and provident effectivity of which the eager and interested ego is not capable. It is when this identification and this self-merging are complete that the divine centre in the world is ready. Purified, liberated, plastic, illumined, it can begin to serve as a means for the direct action of a supreme Power in the larger Yoga of humanity or superhumanity, of the earth's spiritual progression or its transformation.

Always indeed it is the higher Power that acts. Our sense of personal effort and aspiration comes from the attempt of the egoistic mind to identify itself in a wrong and imperfect way with the workings of the divine Force. It persists in applying to experience on a supernormal plane the ordinary terms of mentality which it applies to its normal experiences in the world. In the world we act with the sense of egoism; we claim the universal forces that work in us as our own; we claim as the effect of our personal will, wisdom, force, virtue the selective, formative, progressive action of the Transcendent in this frame of mind, life and body. Enlightenment brings to us the knowledge that the ego is only an instrument; we begin to perceive and feel that these things are our own in the sense that they belong to our supreme and integral Self, one with the Transcendent, not to the instrumental ego. Our limitations and distortions are our contribution to the working; the true power in it is the Divine's. When the human ego realises that its will is a tool, its wisdom ignorance and childishness, its power an infant's groping, its virtue a pretentious impurity, and learns to trust itself to that which transcends it, that is its salvation. The apparent freedom and self-assertion of our personal being to which we are so profoundly attached, conceal a most pitiable subjection to a thousand suggestions, impulsions, forces which we have made extraneous to our little person. Our ego, boasting of freedom, is at every moment the slave, toy and puppet of countless beings, powers, forces, influences in universal Nature. The self-abnegation of the ego in the Divine is its self-fulfilment; its surrender to that which transcends it is its liberation from bonds and limits and its perfect freedom.

But still, in the practical development, each of the three stages has its necessity and utility and must be given its time or its place. It will not do, it cannot be safe or effective to begin with the last and highest alone. It would not be the right course, either, to leap prematurely from one to another. For even if from the beginning we recognise in mind and heart the Supreme, there are elements of the nature which long prevent the recognition from becoming realisation. But without realisation our mental belief cannot become a dynamic reality; it is still only a figure of knowledge, not a living truth, an idea, not yet a power. And even if realisation has begun, it may be dangerous to imagine or to assume too soon that we are altogether in the hands of the Supreme or are acting as his instrument. That assumption may introduce a calamitous falsity; it may produce a helpless inertia or, magnifying the movements of the ego with the Divine Name, it may disastrously distort and ruin the whole course of the Yoga. There is a period, more or less prolonged, of internal effort and struggle in which the individual will has to reject the darkness and distortions of the lower nature and to put itself resolutely or vehemently on the side of the divine Light. The mental energies, the heart's emotions, the vital desires, the very physical being have to be compelled into the right attitude or trained to admit and answer to the right influences. It is only then, only when this has been truly done, that the surrender of the lower to the higher can be effected, because the sacrifice has become acceptable.

The personal will of the sadhaka has first to seize on the egoistic energies and turn them towards the light and the right; once turned, he has still to train them to recognise that always, always to accept, always to follow that. Progressing, he learns, still using the personal will, personal effort, personal energies, to employ them as representatives of the higher Power and in conscious obedience to the higher Influence. Progressing yet farther, his will, effort, energy become no longer personal and separate, but activities of that higher Power and Influence at work in the individual. But there is still a sort of gulf or distance which necessitates an obscure process of transit, not always accurate, sometimes even very distorting, between the divine Origin and the emerging human current. At the end of the progress, with the progressive disappearance of egoism and impurity and ignorance, this last separation is removed; all in the individual becomes the divine working.

*   *   *

As the supreme Shastra of the integral Yoga is the eternal Veda secret in the heart of every man, so its supreme Guide and Teacher is the inner Guide, the World-Teacher, *jagad-guru*, secret within us. It is he who destroys our darkness by the resplendent light of his knowledge; that light becomes within us the increasing glory of his own self-revelation. He discloses progressively in us his own nature of freedom, bliss, love, power, immortal being. He sets above us his divine example as our ideal and transforms the lower existence into a reflection of that which it contemplates. By the inpouring of his own influence and presence into us he enables the individual being to attain to identity with the universal and transcendent.

What is his method and his system? He has no method and every method. His system is a natural organisation of the highest processes and movements of which the nature is capable. Applying themselves even to the pettiest details and to the actions the most insignificant in their appearance with as much care and thoroughness as to the greatest, they in the end lift all into the Light and transform all. For in his Yoga there is nothing too small to be used and nothing too great to be attempted. As the servant and disciple of the Master has no business with pride or egoism because all is done for him from above, so also he has no right to despond because of his personal deficiencies or the stumblings of his nature. For the Force that works in him is impersonal – or superpersonal – and infinite.

The full recognition of this inner Guide, Master of the Yoga, lord, light, enjoyer and goal of all sacrifice and effort, is of the utmost importance in the path of integral perfection. It is immaterial whether he is first seen as an impersonal Wisdom, Love and Power behind all things, as an Absolute manifesting in the relative and attracting it, as one's highest Self and the highest Self of all, as a Divine Person within us and in the world, in one of his – or her – numerous forms and names or as the ideal which the mind conceives. In the end we perceive that he is all and more than all these things together. The mind's door of entry to the conception of him must necessarily vary according to the past evolution and the present nature.

This inner Guide is often veiled at first by the very intensity of our personal effort and by the ego's preoccupation with itself and its aims. As we gain in clarity and the turmoil of egoistic effort gives place to a calmer self-knowledge, we recognise the source of the growing light within us. We recognise it retrospectively as we realise how all our obscure and conflicting movements have been determined towards an end that we only now begin to perceive, how even before our entrance into the path of the Yoga the evolution of our life has been designedly led towards its turning point. For now we begin to understand the sense of our struggles and efforts, successes and failures. At last we are able to seize the meaning of our ordeals and sufferings and can appreciate the help that was given us by all that hurt and resisted and the utility of our very falls and stumblings. We recognise this divine leading afterwards, not retrospectively but immediately, in the moulding of our thoughts by a transcendent Seer, of our will and actions by an all-embracing Power, of our emotional life by an all-attracting and all-assimilating Bliss and Love. We recognise it too in a more personal relation that from the first touched us or at the last seizes us; we feel the eternal presence of a supreme Master, Friend, Lover, Teacher. We recognise it in the essence of our being as that develops into likeness and oneness with a greater and wider existence; for we perceive that this miraculous development is not the result of our own efforts; an eternal Perfection is moulding us into its own image. One who is the Lord or Ishwara of the Yogic philosophies, the Guide in the conscious being (*caitya guru* or *antaryāmin*), the Absolute of the thinker, the Unknowable of the Agnostic, the universal Force of the materialist, the supreme Soul and the supreme Shakti, the One who is differently named and imaged by the religions, is the Master of our Yoga.

To see, know, become and fulfil this One in our inner selves and in all our outer nature, was always the secret goal and becomes now the conscious purpose of our embodied existence. To be conscious of him in all parts of our being and equally in all that the dividing mind sees as outside our being, is the consummation of the individual consciousness. To be possessed by him and possess him in ourselves and in all things is the term of all empire and mastery. To enjoy him in all experience of passivity and activity, of peace and of power, of unity and of difference is the happiness which the *jīva*, the individual soul manifested in the world, is obscurely seeking. This is the entire definition of the aim of integral Yoga; it is the rendering in personal experience of the truth which universal Nature has hidden in herself and which she travails to discover. It is the conversion of the human soul into the divine soul and of natural life into divine living.

* * *

The surest way towards this integral fulfilment is to find the Master of the secret who dwells within us, open ourselves constantly to the divine Power which is also the divine Wisdom and Love and trust to it to effect the conversion. But it is difficult for the egoistic consciousness to do this at all at the beginning. And, if done at all, it is still difficult to do it perfectly and in every strand of our nature. It is difficult at first because our egoistic habits of thought, of sensation, of feeling block up the avenues by which we can arrive at the perception that is needed. It is difficult afterwards because the faith, the surrender, the courage requisite in this path are not easy to the ego-clouded soul. The divine working is not the working which the egoistic mind desires or approves;

for it uses error in order to arrive at truth, suffering in order to arrive at bliss, imperfection in order to arrive at perfection. The ego cannot see where it is being led; it revolts against the leading, loses confidence, loses courage. These failings would not matter; for the divine Guide within is not offended by our revolt, not discouraged by our want of faith or repelled by our weakness; he has the entire love of the mother and the entire patience of the teacher. But by withdrawing our assent from the guidance we lose the consciousness, though not all the actuality – not, in any case, the eventuality – of its benefit. And we withdraw our assent because we fail to distinguish our higher Self from the lower through which he is preparing his self-revelation. As in the world, so in ourselves, we cannot see God because of his workings and, especially, because he works in us through our nature and not by a succession of arbitrary miracles. Man demands miracles that he may have faith; he wishes to be dazzled in order that he may see. And this impatience, this ignorance may turn into a great danger and disaster if, in our revolt against the divine leading, we call in another distorting Force more satisfying to our impulses and desires and ask it to guide us and give it the Divine Name.

But while it is difficult for man to believe in something unseen within himself, it is easy for him to believe in something which he can image as extraneous to himself. The spiritual progress of most human beings demands an extraneous support, an object of faith outside us. It needs an external image of God; or it needs a human representative, – Incarnation, Prophet or Guru; or it demands both and receives them. For according to the need of the human soul the Divine manifests himself as deity, as human divine or in simple humanity – using that thick disguise, which so successfully conceals the Godhead, for a means of transmission of his guidance.

The Hindu discipline of spirituality provides for this need of the soul by the conceptions of the Ishta Devata, the Avatar and the Guru. By the Ishta Devata, the chosen deity, is meant, – not some inferior Power, but a name and form of the transcendent and universal Godhead. Almost all religions either have as their base or make use of some such name and form of the Divine. Its necessity for the human soul is evident. God is the All and more than the All. But that which is more than the All, how shall man conceive? And even the All is at first too hard for him; for he himself in his active consciousness is a limited and selective formation and can open himself only to that which is in harmony with his limited nature. There are things in the All which are too hard for his comprehension or seem too terrible to his sensitive emotions and cowering sensations. Or, simply, he cannot conceive as the Divine, cannot approach or cannot recognise something that is too much out of the circle of his ignorant or partial conceptions. It is necessary for him to conceive God in his own image or in some form that is beyond himself but consonant with his highest tendencies and seizable by his feelings or his intelligence. Otherwise it would be difficult for him to come into contact and communion with the Divine.

Even then his nature calls for a human intermediary

so that he may feel the Divine in something entirely close to his own humanity and sensible in a human influence and example. This call is satisfied by the Divine manifest in a human appearance, the Incarnation, the Avatar – Krishna, Christ, Buddha. Or if this is too hard for him to conceive, the Divine represents himself through a less marvellous intermediary, – Prophet or Teacher. For many who cannot conceive or are unwilling to accept the Divine Man, are ready to open themselves to the supreme man, terming him not incarnation but world-teacher or divine representative.

This also is not enough; a living influence, a living example, a present instruction is needed. For it is only the few who can make the past Teacher and his teaching, the past Incarnation and his example and influence a living force in their lives. For this need also the Hindu discipline provides in the relation of the Guru and the disciple. The Guru may sometimes be the Incarnation or World-Teacher, but it is sufficient that he should represent to the disciple the divine wisdom, convey to him something of the divine ideal or make him feel the realised relation of the human soul with the Eternal.

The sadhaka of the integral Yoga will make use of all these aids according to his nature; but it is necessary that he should shun their limitations and cast from himself that exclusive tendency of egoistic mind which cries, "My God, my Incarnation, my Prophet, my Guru," and opposes it to all other realisation in a sectarian or a fanatical spirit. All sectarianism, all fanaticism must be shunned; for it is inconsistent with the integrity of the divine realisation.

On the contrary, the sadhaka of the integral Yoga will not be satisfied until he has included all other names and forms of Deity in his own conception, seen his own Ishta Devata in all others, unified all Avatars in the unity of Him who descends in the Avatar, welded the truth in all teachings into the harmony of the Eternal Wisdom.

Nor should he forget the aim of these external aids which is to awaken his soul to the Divine within him. Nothing has been finally accomplished if that has not been accomplished. It is not sufficient to worship Krishna, Christ or Buddha without, if there is not the revealing and the formation of the Buddha, the Christ or Krishna in ourselves. And all other aids equally have no other purpose; each is a bridge between man's unconverted state and the revelation of the Divine within him.

* * *

The Teacher of the integral Yoga will follow as far as he may the method of the Teacher within us. He will lead the disciple through the nature of the disciple. Teaching, example, influence, – these are the three instruments of the Guru. But the wise Teacher will not seek to impose himself or his opinions on the passive acceptance of the receptive mind; he will throw in only what is productive and sure as a seed which will grow under the divine fostering within. He will seek to awaken much more than to instruct; he will aim at the growth of the faculties and the experiences by a natural process and free expansion. He will give a method as an aid, as a utilisable device, not as an imperative formula or a fixed routine. And he will be on his guard against any turning of the means into a limitation, against the mechanising of process. His whole business is to awaken the divine light and set working the divine force of which he himself is only a means and an aid, a body or a channel.

The example is more powerful than the instruction; but it is not the example of the outward acts nor that of the personal character, which is of most importance. These have their place and their utility; but what will most stimulate aspiration in others is the central fact of the divine realisation within him governing his whole life and inner state and all his activities. This is the universal and essential element; the rest belongs to individual person and circumstance. It is this dynamic realisation that the Sadhaka must feel and reproduce in himself according to his own nature; he need not strive after an imitation from outside which may well be sterilising rather than productive of right and natural fruits.

Influence is more important than example. Influence is not the outward authority of the Teacher over his disciple, but the power of his contact, of his presence, of the nearness of his soul to the soul of another, infusing into it, even though in silence, that which he himself is and possesses. This is the supreme sign of the Master. For the greatest Master is much less a Teacher than a Presence pouring the divine consciousness and its constituting light and power and purity and bliss into all who are receptive around him.

And it shall also be a sign of the teacher of the integral

Yoga that he does not arrogate to himself Guruhood in a humanly vain and self-exalting spirit. His work, if he has one, is a trust from above, he himself a channel, a vessel or a representative. He is a man helping his brothers, a child leading children, a Light kindling other lights, an awakened Soul awakening souls, at highest a Power or Presence of the Divine calling to him other powers of the Divine.

* * *

The sadhaka who has all these aids is sure of his goal. Even a fall will be for him only a means of rising and death a passage towards fulfilment. For once on this path, birth and death become only processes in the development of his being and the stages of his journey.

Time is the remaining aid needed for the effectivity of the process. Time presents itself to human effort as an enemy or a friend, as a resistance, a medium or an instrument. But always it is really the instrument of the soul.

Time is a field of circumstances and forces meeting and working out a resultant progression whose course it measures. To the ego it is a tyrant or a resistance, to the Divine an instrument. Therefore, while our effort is personal, Time appears as a resistance, for it presents to us all the obstruction of the forces that conflict with our own. When the divine working and the personal are combined in our consciousness, it appears as a medium and a condition. When the two become one, it appears as a servant and instrument.

The ideal attitude of the sadhaka towards Time is to

have an endless patience as if he had all eternity for his fulfilment and yet to develop the energy that shall realise now and with an ever-increasing mastery and pressure of rapidity till it reaches the miraculous instantaneousness of the supreme divine Transformation.

SELECTED LETTERS

A Letter to a Disciple

To find the Divine is indeed the first reason for seeking the spiritual Truth and the spiritual life; it is the one thing indispensable and all the rest is nothing without it. The Divine once found, to manifest Him, – that is, first of all to transform one's own limited consciousness into the Divine Consciousness, to live in the infinite Peace, Light, Love, Strength, Bliss, to become that in one's essential nature and, as a consequence, to be its vessel, channel, instrument in one's active nature. To bring into activity the principle of oneness on the material plane or to work for humanity is a mental mistranslation of the Truth – these things cannot be the first true object of spiritual seeking. We must find the Self, the Divine, then only can we know what is the work the Self or the Divine demands from us. Until then our life and action can only be a help or means towards finding the Divine and it ought not to have any other purpose. As we grow in the inner consciousness, or as the spiritual Truth of the Divine grows in us, our life and action must indeed more and more flow from that, be one with that. But to decide beforehand by our limited mental conceptions what they must be is to hamper the growth of the spiritual Truth within. As that grows we shall feel the Divine Light and Truth, the Divine Power and Force, the Divine Purity and Peace working within us, dealing with our actions as well as our consciousness, making use of them to reshape us into the Divine Image, removing the dross, substituting the pure gold of the Spirit. Only when the Divine Presence is there in us always and the consciousness transformed, can we have the right to say that we are ready to manifest the Divine on the material plane. To hold up a mental ideal or principle and impose that on the inner working brings the danger of limiting ourselves to a mental realisation or of impeding or even falsifying by a half-way formation the true growth into the full communion and union with the Divine and the free and intimate outflowing of His will in our life. This is a mistake of orientation to which the mind of today is especially prone. It is far better to approach the Divine for the Peace or Light or Bliss that the realisation of Him gives than to bring in these minor things which can divert us from the one thing needful. The divinisation of the material life also as well as the inner life is part of what we see as the Divine Plan, but it can only be fulfilled by an outflowing of the inner realisation, something that grows from within outwards, not by the working out of a mental principle.

You have asked what is the discipline to be followed in order to convert the mental seeking into a living spiritual experience. The first necessity is the practice of concentration of your consciousness within yourself. The ordinary human mind has an activity on the surface which veils the real Self. But there is another, a hidden consciousness within behind the surface one in which we can become aware of the real Self and of a larger deeper truth of nature, can realise the Self and liberate and transform the nature. To quiet the surface mind and begin to live within is the object of this concentration. Of this true consciousness other than the superficial there are two main centres, one in the heart (not the physical heart, but the cardiac centre in the middle of the chest), one in the head. The concentration in the heart opens within and by following this inward opening and going deep one becomes aware of the soul or psychic being, the divine element in the individual. This being unveiled begins to come forward, to govern the nature, to turn it and all its movements towards the Truth, towards the Divine, and to call down into it all that is above. It brings the consciousness of the Presence, the dedication of the being to the Highest and invites the descent into our nature of a greater Force and Consciousness which is waiting above us. To concentrate in the heart centre with the offering of oneself to the Divine and the aspiration for this inward opening and for the Presence in the heart is the first way and, if it can be done, the natural beginning; for its result once obtained makes the spiritual path far more easy and safe than if one begins the other way.

That other way is the concentration in the head, in the mental centre. This, if it brings about the silence of the surface mind, opens up an inner, larger, deeper mind within which is more capable of receiving spiritual experience and spiritual knowledge. But once concentrated here one must open the silent mental consciousness upward to all that is above mind. After a time one feels the consciousness rising upward and in the end it rises beyond the lid which has so long kept it tied in the body and finds a centre above the head where it is liberated into the Infinite. There it begins to come into contact with the universal Self, the Divine Peace, Light, Power, Knowledge, Bliss, to enter into that and become that, to feel the descent of these things into the nature. To concentrate in the head with the aspiration for quietude in the mind and the realisation of the Self and Divine above is the second way of concentration. It is important, however, to remember that the concentration of the consciousness in the head is only a preparation for its rising to the centre above; otherwise, one may get shut up in one's own mind and its experiences or at best attain only to a reflection of the Truth above instead of rising into the spiritual transcendence to live there. For some the mental concentration is easier, for some the concentration in the heart centre; some are capable of doing both alternately – but to begin with the heart centre, if one can do it, is the more desirable.

The other side of discipline is with regard to the activities of the nature, of the mind, of the life-self or vital, of the physical being. Here the principle is to accord the nature with the inner realisation so that one may not be divided into two discordant parts. There are here several disciplines or processes possible. One is to offer all the activities to the Divine and call for the inner guidance and the taking up of one's nature by a Higher Power. If there is the inward soul-opening, if the psychic being comes forward, then there is no great difficulty – there comes with it a psychic discrimination, a constant intimation, finally a governance which discloses and quietly and patiently removes all imperfections, brings the right mental and vital movements and reshapes the physical consciousness also. Another method is to stand back detached from the movements of the mind, life, physical being, to regard their activities as only a habitual formation of general Nature in the individual imposed on us by past workings, not as any part of our real being; in proportion as one succeeds in this, becomes detached, sees mind and its activities as not oneself, life and its activities as not oneself, the body and its activities as not oneself, one becomes aware of an inner Being within us – inner mental, inner vital, inner physical – silent, calm, unbound, unattached which reflects the true Self above and can be its direct representative; from this inner silent Being proceeds a rejection of all that is to be rejected, an acceptance only of what can be kept and transformed, an inmost Will to perfection or a call to the Divine Power to do at each step what is necessary for the change of the Nature. It can also open mind, life and body to the inmost psychic entity and its guiding influence or its direct guidance. In most cases these two methods emerge and work together and finally fuse into one. But one can begin with either, the one that one feels most natural and easy to follow.

Finally, in all difficulties where personal effort is hampered, the help of the Teacher can intervene and bring about what is needed for the realisation or for the immediate step that is necessary.

Extracts from Letters

I

...the principle of this Yoga is not perfection of the human nature as it is but a psychic and spiritual transformation of all the parts of the being through the action of an inner consciousness and then of a higher consciousness which works on them, throws out their old movements or changes them into the image of its own and so transmutes lower into higher nature. It is not so much the perfection of the intellect as a transcendence of it, a transformation of the mind, the substitution of a larger greater principle of knowledge – and so with all the rest of the being.

This is a slow and difficult process; the road is long and it is hard to establish even the necessary basis. The old existing nature resists and obstructs and difficulties rise one after another and repeatedly till they are overcome.

II

In our yoga the Nirvana is the beginning of the higher Truth, as it is the passage from the Ignorance to the higher Truth. The Ignorance has to be extinguished in order that the Truth may manifest.

III

What we are doing, if and when we succeed, will be a beginning, not a completion. It is the foundation of a new consciousness on earth – a consciousness with infinite possibilities of manifestation. The eternal progression is in the manifestation and beyond it there is no progression.

If the redemption of the soul from the physical vesture be the object, then there is no need of supramentalisation. Spiritual Mukti and Nirvana are sufficient. If the object is to rise to supraphysical planes, then also there is no need of supramentalisation. One can enter into some heaven above by devotion to the Lord of that heaven. But that is no progression. The other worlds are typal worlds, each fixed in its own kind and type and law. Evolution takes place on the earth and therefore the earth is the proper field for progression. The beings of the other worlds do not progress from one world to another. They remain fixed to their own type.

The purely monistic Vedantist says, all is Brahman, life is a dream, an unreality, only Brahman exists. One has Nirvana or Mukti, then one lives only till the body falls – after that there is no such thing as life.

They do not believe in transformation, because mind, life and body are an ignorance, an illusion – the only reality is the featureless relationless Self or Brahman. Life is a thing of relations; in the pure Self, all life and relations disappear. What would be the use or the possibility of transforming an illusion that can never be anything else (however transformed) than an illusion? There is no such thing for them as a "Nirvanic life".

It is only some yogas that aim at a transformation of any kind except that of ignorance into knowledge. The idea varies, – sometimes a divine knowledge or power or else a divine purity or an ethical perfection or a divine love.

What has to be overcome is the opposition of the Ignorance that does not want the transformation of the nature. If that can be overcome, then old spiritual ideas will not form an obstacle.

It is not intended to supramentalise humanity at large, but to establish the principle of the supramental consciousness in the earth-evolution. If that is done, all that is needed will be evolved by the supramental Power itself. It is not therefore important that the mission should be widespread. What is important is that the thing should be done at all in however small a number; that is the only difficulty.

If the transformation of the body is complete, that means no subjection to death – it does not mean that one will be bound to keep the same body for all time. One creates a new body for oneself when one wants to change, but how it will be done cannot be said now. The present method is by physical birth – some occultists suppose that a time will come when that will not be necessary – but the question must be left for the supramental evolution to decide.

The questions about the supermind cannot be answered profitably now. Supermind cannot be described in terms that the mind will understand, because the terms will be mental and mind will understand them in a mental way and mental sense and miss their true import. It would therefore be a waste of time and energy which should be devoted to the preliminary work – psychicisation and spiritualisation of the being and nature without which no supramentalisation is possible. Let the whole dynamic nature led by the psychic make itself full of the dynamic spiritual light, peace, purity, knowledge, force; let it afterwards get experience of the intermediate spiritual planes and know, feel and act in their sense; then it will be possible to speak last of the supramental transformation.

IV

In the supramental consciousness, there are no problems – the problem is created by the division set up by the Mind. The supramental sees the Truth as a single whole and everything falls into its place in that whole. The supramental is also spiritual, but the old yogas reach Sachchidananda through the spiritualised mind and depart into the eternally static oneness of Sachchidananda or rather pure Sat (Existence), absolute and eternal or else a pure Non-existence, absolute and eternal. Ours having realised Sachchidananda in the spiritualised mind plane proceeds to realise it in the supramental plane.

The supreme supracosmic Sachchidananda is above all. Supermind may be described as its power of self-awareness and world-awareness, the world being known as within itself and not outside. So to live consciously in the supreme Sachchidananda one must pass through the supermind. If one is in the supracosmic apart from the manifestation, there is no place for problems or solutions. If one lives in the transcendence and the cosmic view at the same time, that can only be by the supramental consciousness in the supreme Sachchidananda consciousness – so why should the question arise? Why should there be a difference between the supreme Sachchidananda version of the cosmos and the supermind's version of it? Your difficulty probably comes from thinking of both in terms of the mind.

The supermind is an entirely different consciousness not only from the spiritualised Mind, but from the planes above spiritualised Mind which intervene between it and the supramental plane. Once one passes beyond overmind to supermind, one enters into a consciousness to which the norms of the other planes do not at all apply and in which the same Truth, e.g. Sachchidananda and truth of this universe, is seen in quite a different way and has a different dynamic consequence. This necessarily results from the fact that supermind has an indivisible knowledge, while overmind proceeds by union in division and Mind by division taking division as the first fact, for that is the natural process of its knowledge.

In all planes the essential experience of Sachchidananda, pure Existence, Consciousness, Bliss is the same and Mind is often contented with it as the sole Truth and dismisses all else as part of the grand Illusion, but there is also a dynamic experience of the Divine or of

Existence (e.g. as One and Many, Personal and Impersonal, the Infinite and Finite, etc.) which is essential for the integral knowledge. The dynamic experience is not the same in the lower planes as in the higher, in the intermediate spiritual planes and in the supramental. In these the oppositions can only be put together and harmonised, in the supermind they fuse together and are inseparably one; that makes an enormous difference.

The universe is dynamism, movement – the essential experience of Sachchidananda apart from the dynamism and movement is static. The full dynamic truth of Sachchidananda and the universe and its consequence cannot be grasped by any other consciousness than the supermind, because the instrumentation in all other (lower) planes is inferior and there is therefore a disparity between the fullness of the static experience and the incompleteness of the dynamic power, knowledge, result of the inferior light and power of other planes. This is the reason why the consciousness of the other spiritual planes, even if it descends, can make no radical change in the earth-consciousness, it can only modify or enrich it. The radical transformation needs the descent of a supramental power and nature.

One cannot speak of two classes of Sachchidananda, for Sachchidananda is the same always – but the knowledge of Sachchidananda and the universe differs according to the degree of the consciousness which has the experience.

The personal realisation of the Divine may be sometimes with Form, sometimes without Form. Without

Form, it is the Presence of the living Divine Person, felt in everything. With Form, it comes with the image of the One to whom worship is offered. The Divine can always manifest himself in a form to the bhakta or seeker. One sees him in the form in which one worships or seeks him or in a form suitable to the Divine Personality who is the object of the adoration. How it manifests depends on many things and it is too various to be reduced to a single rule. Sometimes it is in the heart that the Presence with the form is seen, sometimes in any of the other centres, sometimes above and guiding from there, sometimes it is seen outside and in front as if an embodied Person. Its advantages are an intimate relation and constant guidance or if felt or seen within, a very strong and concrete realisation of the constant Presence. But one must be very sure of the purity of one's adoration and seeking – for the disadvantage of this kind of embodied relation is that other Forces can imitate the Form or counterfeit the voice and the guidance and this gets more force if it is associated with a constructed image which is not the true thing. Several have been misled in this way because pride, vanity or desire was strong in them and robbed them of the finer psychic perception that is not mental and can at once turn the Mother's light on such misleadings or errors.